HOLLYWOOD HULK HOGAN
The Story of Terry Bollea

A Real-Life Reader Biography

Susan Zannos

Mitchell Lane Publishers, Inc.
P.O. Box 200 • Childs, Maryland 21916

Second Printing

Real-Life Reader Biographies

Selena	Robert Rodriguez	Mariah Carey	Rafael Palmeiro
Tommy Nuñez	Trent Dimas	Cristina Saralegui	Andres Galarraga
Oscar De La Hoya	Gloria Estefan	Jimmy Smits	Mary Joe Fernandez
Cesar Chavez	Chuck Norris	Sinbad	Paula Abdul
Vanessa Williams	Celine Dion	Mia Hamm	Sammy Sosa
Brandy	Michelle Kwan	Rosie O'Donnell	Shania Twain
Garth Brooks	Jeff Gordon	Mark McGwire	Salma Hayek
Sheila E.	**Hollywood Hogan**	Ricky Martin	Britney Spears
Arnold Schwarzenegger	Jennifer Lopez	Kobe Bryant	Derek Jeter
Steve Jobs	Sandra Bullock	Julia Roberts	Robin Williams
Jennifer Love Hewitt	Keri Russell	Sarah Michelle Gellar	Liv Tyler
Melissa Joan Hart	Drew Barrymore	Alicia Silverstone	Katie Holmes
Winona Ryder	Alyssa Milano		

Library of Congress Cataloging-in-Publication Data
Zannos, Susan.
     Hollywood Hulk Hogan: the story of Terry Bollea/Susan Zannos.
         p. cm. — (A real-life reader biography)
     Includes index.
     Summary: A biography of the professional wrestler, Terry Bollea, better known as Hulk Hogan or Hollywood Hogan, from his childhood in Florida through his early wrestling career to his show business success.
      ISBN 1-58415-021-1
     1. Hogan, Hulk, 1955- Juvenile literature. 2. Wrestlers—United States Biography Juvenile literature. [1. Hogan, Hulk, 1955- . 2. Wrestlers.] I. Title. II. Series.
GV1196.H64Z36 2000
796.812'092—dc21
[B]—DC21
                                                        99-28667
                                                                 CIP

ABOUT THE AUTHOR: Susan Zannos has taught at all levels, from preschool to college, in Mexico, Greece, Italy, Russia, and Lithuania, as well as in the United States. She has published a mystery **Trust the Liar** (Walker and Co.) and **Human Types: Essence and the Enneagram** was published by Samuel Weiser in 1997. She has written several books for children, including **Paula Abdul** and **Cesar Chavez** (Mitchell Lane).

PHOTO CREDITS: cover: Lisa Rose/Globe Photos; p. 4 Scott Palmer/Allsport; p. 6 Elsa Hasch/Allsport; p. 20, 24 Reuters/Peter Jones/Archive Photos; p. 23, 26 Raul De Molina/Shooting Star; p. 28 Ron Davis/ Shooting Star.

ACKNOWLEDGMENTS: The following story has been thoroughly researched, and to the best of our knowledge, represents a true story. Though we try to authorize every biography that we publish, for various reasons, this is not always possible. This story is not authorized nor endorsed by Hollywood Hulk Hogan.

Table of Contents

4

Chapter 1
Most Popular Wrestler

When Hollywood Hogan comes out of his dressing room and starts down the aisle toward the ring, the crowd goes wild. Loud music pulses through the huge auditorium filled with tens of thousands of his fans. Many of the spectators are children. When Hogan climbs into the ring, he rips off his tank top and throws it to his fans. He struts around the ring. He rolls his eyes and bares his teeth in a threatening smile. He flexes his

Hogan climbs into the ring, rips off his tank top and throws it to his fans.

huge muscles. The audience cheers and cheers.

Hollywood Hogan is 6′8″ tall and weighs nearly 300 pounds. He is the best known wrestler who ever lived. He has made professional wrestling popular with millions and millions of people all over the world.

At the NCW Bash at the Beach held in 1998 at Cox Arena in San Diego, CA, Hogan fought "Mailman" Karl Malone.

The huge wrestler wasn't always known as Hulk Hogan. His mom and dad named him Terry Gene Bollea when he was born on August 11, 1953, in Augusta, Georgia. Soon after he was born the family moved to Tampa, Florida.

Terry's dad, Pete Bollea, was a construction foreman. His mom, Ruth, was a homemaker and also a dance teacher. "I guess Terry gets a lot of his showmanship from me," she later said. Terry was the youngest boy in the family. His oldest brother, Kenneth, grew up to be a colonel in the Air Force. His other brother, Allan, died when Terry was very young.

Hulk Hogan is really Terry Gene Bollea.

Terry was big even when he was a newborn, weighing over 10 pounds. From this healthy start, he continued to grow rapidly. By the time Terry was 12 years old, he weighed nearly 200 pounds. But he was not fat, he was big and strong. Terry loved to use his strength, and he began wrestling in school. Unfortunately, he began fighting outside of school as well.

When he was 14 years old, Terry was arrested for street fighting. He was sent to the Florida Sheriffs Boys Ranch, a special school for teenage boys who had problems with the law. The school tried to help the teens before they got into serious trouble. In Terry's case, it worked. While at the Boys Ranch, he became a devout Christian. When he left the school, he vowed to live a good life and stay out of trouble.

Terry studied business at a community college, and went on to study at the University of South Florida. He left college and took a job as a stevedore (someone who helps load and unload ships). A man has to be very strong to be a stevedore, so Terry Bollea was good at the job. But it was not what he wanted to do with his life.

Two professional wrestlers, Jack and Jerry Brisco, owned the local gym where Terry worked out lifting weights. The Brisco brothers were impressed with the strong young man, and one day they asked him if he'd ever thought of becoming a wrestler. Terry Bollea answered, "I've wanted to be one all my life."

Terry was sent to the Florida Sheriffs Boys Ranch where he turned his life around.

Chapter 2
Learning the Ropes

Terry Bollea worked hard learning to be a professional wrestler. He trained with the Brisco brothers for several months before he had his first bout. The crowd at this 1978 match recognized that they were seeing someone special. "Nobody had a clue who this was," Jerry Brisco remembered, "but they were cheering him like he was already a superstar."

Terry spent a few months wrestling on small circuits in the

Terry trained with the Brisco brothers, learning to be a wrestler.

Southeast, earning only $125 a week for seven nights of work. But he was learning the ropes of wrestling. When the Brisco brothers introduced him to a Japanese wrestler and trainer named Hiro Matsuda, Terry learned a lot more. Around this time Terry changed his name to Terry "The Hulk" Boulder.

He changed his name again when he started wrestling for a bigger wrestling league, the Continental Wrestling Association (CWA). In December 1979, using the name Sterling Golden, he won the CWA's Southeastern championship. Terry wasn't earning much money yet, but he was starting to be noticed. The promoters (people in charge of the wrestling organizations) saw that fans liked the young wrestler and wanted to watch him win.

Soon, he changed his name to Terry "The Hulk" Boulder.

One of the biggest of these promoters, Vincent McMahon Sr., was owner of the powerful World Wrestling Federation (WWF). The World Wrestling Federation was one of the biggest associations in the United States. McMahon wanted Terry Bollea to wrestle for the WWF. He suggested that Terry change his name again, this time to Hulk Hogan. At that time, a television show called *The Incredible Hulk* was popular, and McMahon thought Terry looked like the star of that show.

But Hulk Hogan would not be popular right away. In fact, McMahon wanted him to be unpopular. Wrestlers are usually cast as either good guys or villains. In wrestling terms, the bad guy in a match is called a "heel." Hulk Hogan was going to be a heel.

Hulk Hogan's first match for the WWF came two days before Terry's 27th birthday, on August 9, 1980. It was a huge event at Shea Stadium in New York, attended by over 50,000 people. Hulk wrestled one of the WWF's biggest stars, Andre the Giant. The 7´5´´ Andre was a fan favorite, and the crowd cheered when he pinned Hogan.

In addition to the thousands of fans at the event, many more watched it on cable television. One person who saw the match was movie star Sylvester Stallone. He was so impressed with Hulk that he offered him a part in a film that he was making, *Rocky III*. It was not a large part. Terry was to play a wrestler named Thunderlips that Sylvester Stallone's character, a boxer named Rocky Balboa, fights in a charity event. After *Rocky III*

In his first match for the WWF, he fought Andre the Giant. Andre was 7' 5" tall.

was released, Terry received a lot of attention for his role in the movie. He thought that one day he might like a career as an actor.

But first, he wanted to become a wrestling champion. After *Rocky III*, Hulk Hogan joined the American Wrestling Association (AWA). He became a star with the AWA. Hogan started wrestling as a "baby face," a term for the good guy in a professional wrestling match. Hulk liked being the good guy better than the villain. "It's nice not to find your tires slashed when you leave the arena," he once commented.

However, even though he was very popular with the AWA's fans, Hulk was not allowed to win the championship. Frustrated, he went to Japan and joined a new wrestling association, the International

When Hogan joined the American Wrestling Association, he wrestled as a baby face (good guy).

Wrestling Grand Prix (IWGP). On June 2, 1983, he defeated Antonio Inoki to become the first IWGP heavyweight champion.

Things were definitely looking up for Hulk Hogan. Back in the United States, a new man was in charge of the World Wrestling Federation. Vince McMahon Jr. had taken over the WWF from his aging father. The younger McMahon saw that fans loved the nice-guy Hulkster. He arranged for Hulk Hogan to challenge for the WWF title.

When he returned to the WWF, Hogan was allowed to challenge for the WWF title.

Chapter 3
Hulkamania

On January 23, 1984, the world of professional wrestling changed forever. On that night, Hulk Hogan defeated the WWF champion, an unpopular wrestler called the Iron Sheik. After Hogan won the WWF title, interest in professional wrestling grew like never before. The increased popularity led to pay-per-view television specials, media coverage, and merchandising of toys, clothes, and other items. This new wave of wrestling popularity was called "Hulkamania."

Hulk Hogan spent 200 days a year on the road, wrestling in arenas across the country. He appeared on 250 television stations that carried the WWF's shows. He made commercials for many products, from children's vitamins and cereal to deodorant. In addition there was a whole line of Hulk Hogan products his fans could buy.

Hulk Hogan and Vince McMahon Jr. had changed the world of professional wrestling. They admitted that the matches were more show business than sport. Not every move in the ring was planned, they said, but the outcomes were not left to chance. Usually, the good guys won.

Even though most fans know pro wrestling matches are planned

Professional wrestling is more show business than sport.

The wrestlers rush around the ring like madmen, bouncing off the ropes, slamming into each other...

in advance, they love the spectacle. The wrestlers growl and threaten each other, scream terrible insults, and seem like they are about to tear each other apart. They rush about the ring like madmen, bouncing off the ropes, slamming into each other, trying to strangle their opponents or pick them up and hurl them to the mat. Actually, most of this is acting. The wrestlers are careful not to really hurt each other badly.

It is up to the one who is getting hit to act as though he is really hurt. When it looks like one man has jumped on another with his entire weight, he is actually catching himself with his knees on the mat, not on his opponent's neck and chest. But the wrestler on the bottom screams and makes faces and jerks his body around as though suffering horribly. When one wrestler seems to be hitting the other in the head, he is actually taking the blow on his own arm which is behind his opponent's head. But the man who is supposed to be hit grabs his head and howls as though in terrible pain.

Fans loved to follow the successes of different wrestlers, and were thrilled at the many rivalries that developed. In one match, held in Ontario, Canada, Hulk Hogan was overpowered by two opponents, Big John Studd and Ken Patera. They held him down and were going to cut his long blond hair. Then a fan jumped into the ring to help the Hulkster. Afterward, Hulk Hogan helped the young man become a wrestler. He called himself Hillbilly Jim, wore farmer's overalls in the ring, and

When one wrestler seems to be hitting the other in the head, he is actually taking the blow on his own arm which is behind his opponent's head.

became one of Hulk Hogan's most popular tag-team partners.

Hulk Hogan was the best-known wrestler in the WWF, and he soon became the most popular wrestler of all time. And he was not just popular in the United States: Hulkamania quickly spread all over

The Ultimate Warrior lifts Hulk Hogan and gets to slam him to the mat during Wrestlemania VI, April 1, 1990.

the world. Huge crowds would come to see him wrestle. In August 1986, more than 74,000 people saw him defend his title against "Mr. Wonderful" Paul Orndorff. In March 1987, over 93,000 people packed the Pontiac Silverdome to watch Hogan keep his title by pinning Andre the Giant. These crowds were much larger than the usual attendance at sporting events. In addition, millions more watched at home on cable television.

Hulk Hogan held the WWF title from 1984 to 1988, when he lost to his longtime rival Andre the Giant. Over the next five years, he won and lost the WWF heavyweight title four times. But by the time he lost the WWF title for the final time, in June 1993, the Hulkster's career seemed to be running out of steam.

Chapter 4
Slammed
to the Mat

By 1990, Hulk Hogan was one of the highest paid enter— tainers in the world.

By 1990, Hulk Hogan was one of the highest paid entertainers in the world. He was making between $5 and $10 million a year. He and his wife, Linda, whom he married in 1984, had two children. Daughter Brooke was born in 1989, and son Nicholas was born in 1990. The happy family lived in a beautiful home near Clearwater, Florida. "I'm in love with my kids, I'm in love with my wife," Hulk Hogan said.

"When there's a negative, I run it right over."

Before long, however, there were problems. The acting career that Hulk Hogan had hoped for after *Rocky III* never worked out. He did make a few movies. In 1989, Hulk took a leave of absence from wrestling to make *No Holds Barred*, a movie about wrestling. In 1991 he made *Suburban Commando*, which got bad reviews and did poorly at the box office. Another film in 1993, *Mr. Nanny*, was also a failure.

Hulk Hogan has a beautiful home near Clearwater, Florida, where he loves to play on his boat.

Hulk Hogan raises the arm and points to the new WWF champion, the Ultimate Warrior.

There were problems with his wrestling career, too. Vince McMahon, head of the WWF told Hulk that he had to give up the title belt. McMahon wanted to pass the championship to a young challenger, Bret Hart. He wanted

Hulk Hogan to be an advisor to other wrestlers. Hogan refused, but he was forced to give up the championship anyway. He went back to Japan where he continued to be very popular.

But the worst was yet to come. In 1994 Vince McMahon was accused of giving steroids to his wrestlers. Steroids are drugs that help athletes develop bigger muscles. They are dangerous to use and are illegal unless a doctor prescribes them. In the 1980s, many athletes had taken steroids, not realizing the drugs could damage their health.

Hulk Hogan was one of the wrestlers who had to testify in court. He admitted that he had used steroids. After the trial, many people thought that Hulk Hogan's career was over.

Hulk Hogan admitted he had taken steroids, not realizing the drugs could damage his health.

The situation was like one of Hogan's wrestling matches. It looked like the champ was defeated. Could Hulk Hogan bounce back?

Hulk Hogan loves his "bad boy" image.

Chapter 5
Hollywood Hogan

After taking a year to wrestle in Japan, Hulk Hogan decided not to return to the WWF. Instead, in 1994 he joined a new association called World Championship Wrestling (WCW). WCW had been set up by media mogul Ted Turner. Hulk Hogan quickly became the WCW's biggest star. Turner also cast him in a television action adventure series, *Thunder in Paradise*, which appeared on Turner's TNT channel during 1994.

In 1994, Hogan joined World Championship Wrestling, which had been set up by Ted Turner.

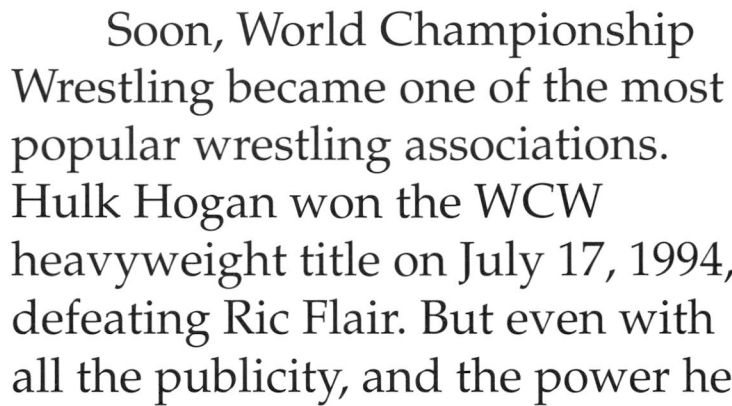

Soon, World Championship Wrestling became one of the most popular wrestling associations. Hulk Hogan won the WCW heavyweight title on July 17, 1994, defeating Ric Flair. But even with all the publicity, and the power he had within the WCW, Hulk Hogan found he had lost the support of his fans. He was even booed. He knew he had to come up with something that would turn his career around.

In 1996 he made another movie, *Santa with Muscles*. Like his earlier films, it

Doesn't he look like Santa with muscles?

was a disaster. But it gave him an idea for a new name: Hollywood Hogan. He also decided to become one of the bad guys. In June 1996, Hollywood Hogan and a group of renegade wrestlers named themselves the New World Order (NWO). The NWO, which now includes Kevin Nash, Eric Bischoff, Buff Bagwell, and Lex Luger, attacked the good-guy wrestlers who had been Hulk Hogan's allies in the 1980s. The fans booed, but thanks to Hollywood Hogan, interest in wrestling was higher than ever.

After he made the movie, *Santa With Muscles*, Hogan decided his new name would be Hollywood Hogan.

The battles between the NWO and the stars of the WCW made World Championship Wrestling the most popular professional wrestling organization in the country. Once more Hogan had been the major force in the forming of a wrestling empire. Professional wrestling not only regained popularity, but attracted even more fans than it had 10 years before.

In July of 1998, Hogan appeared on *The Tonight Show with Jay Leno.* The show received very high ratings. This gave him another idea. He and Eric Bischoff staged a fake takeover of Jay Leno's program one night, and challenged him to "settle in the ring." The tag-team match with Leno later drew national media attention.

Jay Leno isn't the only celebrity that has been lured into the ring for the big WCW events. In Bash at the Beach '98, basketball great Dennis Rodman and Hollywood Hogan were tag-team partners.

Now that he's a bad guy, Hollywood Hogan wears black outfits and dark glasses. His style is

In 1998, Hogan challenged Jay Leno to "settle in the ring."

very, very wicked. He has led the New World Order to become very popular, not only because of their huge wrestling extravaganzas like SuperBrawl, Halloween Havoc, and World War 3, but also because their names and images are used in popular video games.

And what about Terry Bollea, the man who acts the part of Hollywood Hogan, leader of the NWO? Well, he wouldn't want it known, because it would be bad publicity, but he's still just a "baby face" at heart. He's a family man whose wife and children are the most important things in his life. He devotes both time and money to charities that help sick children, and visits many of these children personally. But to his millions of fans, Hollywood Hogan is the heel they love to hate!

Terry Bollea is really just a devoted family man who spends both time and money on charities that help sick children.

Chronology

Index